CW01430552

Acrobat

Acrobat

Poems by Nabaneeta Dev Sen

Introduced and translated from the Bengali
by Nandana Dev Sen

juggernaut

JUGGERNAUT BOOKS
C-I-128, First Floor, Sangam Vihar,
Near Holi Chowk, New Delhi 110080, India

First published in India by Juggernaut Books 2021
Copyright © Nandana Dev Sen 2021
Translation copyright © Nandana Dev Sen 2021

10 9 8 7 6 5 4 3 2 1

P-ISBN: 9789391165758
E-ISBN: 9789391165765

All rights reserved. No part of this publication may be
reproduced, transmitted, or stored in a retrieval system
in any form or by any means without the written
permission of the publisher.

Typeset in Adobe Caslon Pro and Shonar Bangla by
I*Cues*
Printed at Thomson Press India Ltd

For the men I love:
John and Baba

Contents

Sapling of a Heart

Do I Know This Face?

"Every Word a Lifelong Quest"

Poetry and Nabaneeta Dev Sen

I was conceived in the womb of one poet and sired by another.
Poetry, I suspect, was ruling my stars from the very first
moment of my being. I had no way of avoiding its grips.

—Nabaneeta Dev Sen

My mother couldn't remember a time in her life when she did not write poetry. Raised by two celebrated poets, Radharani Debi and Narendra Dev (and named by Rabindranath Tagore), she published her poems in a magazine at age seven, in both Bengali and English. Her first book of poems, *Pratham Pratyay* (*First Confidence*), was greeted with much acclaim the year she turned 21, just before she left for Harvard. She grew to be immensely popular in every genre she chose—fiction or non-fiction, feminist essays or children's books, travelogues or journalism—and her books in prose far outnumbered her poetry collections. And yet, throughout her life, she made no secret of the fact that she would always identify herself as a poet. "No matter what I write, it is always a poet writing," she wrote with her self-proclaimed "poet's immodesty," for "it was in the looking glass of poetry that I saw my face for the first time. Poetry was my first confidence."

Indeed, poetry was not only Nabaneeta's "first confidence"—her first allegiance, her first love—but proved itself, time and again, to be her unwavering life partner. As a child, she cherished the little black notebook Radharani had given her for writing poems, which initiated a lifelong compulsion to carry a "kabitar khata" with her everywhere. Right until the last weeks of her life, Ma kept scribbling lines of poems in her notebook, poems which remained incomplete as much for her ill health as for her incurable perfectionism. She signed the agreement for *Acrobat* with great rejoicing just two weeks before she died. Although my mother had over a hundred books to her credit, our book was going to be, incredibly, her first one published for an international audience. She announced the birth of *Acrobat* with uninhibited excitement in her very last weekly column, one she dictated from bed as she waited to get her strength back.

Ma, always as adored for her spirit as she was for her

words, was characteristically undaunted by the gravity of her illness, although she understood that it was terminal, that there was reason for haste. We started selecting poems for *Acrobat*—a handful of her translated poems had been in circulation for years, but my mother was eager that our book should introduce newer translations, curated from six decades of poetry. So we made a first (and modest) list of poems together, poems that she insisted that I must translate. And that's as far as we got.

I have now translated all the poems on that list, and twice as many more. I've included in *Acrobat* my mother's own stunning translations, her rare English poems (written mostly when she lived in London), and a political poem powerfully translated by my sister Antara for her literary journal, *The Little Magazine*. The collection also contains some of our first translations together, poems that Ma and I had worked on over three decades ago, as well as poems from *Make Up Your Mind*, my translation of her last book of new poetry.

It has taken me a year to complete *Acrobat*—not that long, I suppose, considering that it represents an intricate body of work woven over 60 years—a year in which I have missed her at every word, with every line. There is so much to say about a lifetime of luminous poetry. But if my mother were introducing this book to you herself, as I had fervently hoped she would, I know she would have begun by telling you how deeply she believed in the vital necessity of poetry, and in every freedom it delivers:

> *I speak for poetry as being central to a woman's freedom. Yes, I am partial, I cannot be and do not wish to be objective in this one respect . . . It is not only the printed word that spells inner freedom for us women, there are oral songs composed by village women. They sing their own sorrows and anguish . . . Poetry is a means of our survival, it is a window through which we can breathe.*

As a young wife and scholar shuttling between America and England, Nabaneeta had stopped publishing poetry for a while, focusing instead on her family, and her pioneering research on the oral origins of epic poetry. When her marriage fell apart, she returned to India with two young daughters. Her recent separation and the anticipated divorce—which would be the first of its kind in her social and literary circle in Kolkata—became a scandal that was suffocating for her. But within a year, Nabaneeta published her second book of poems (after a gap of thirteen years), reopening that window through which she could breathe.

Poetry brought Nabaneeta the kind of "freedom" that was most precious to her—the freedom to explore her own broken voice, and to secure her identity in a timid world that initially struggled to find a place for her again. It gave her the freedom to reach out to a large and responsive audience, to discover another kind of love. And till her last days, she stayed strongly connected to her readers: "People feel they can trust me, they feel I will understand. They feel I am of some use to them when they need human warmth . . . They feel I'm a part of their lives, and, in a way, they become a part of mine too. It's a blessing."

Beyond providing Nabaneeta with a devoted readership and a powerful public platform, poetry also paved for her a private route to healing. Poetry allowed her the freedom to unveil her deepest emotions, to "sing her sorrows" or register her dissent, to write off layers of social and linguistic conditioning and write out her heart with no restraint. Throughout her life, poetry empowered Nabaneeta to find and keep her balance during upheavals of every kind, whether it was the ferocity of love or the anxiety of motherhood; the shock of rejection or the grief of bereavement; the despair of communal violence or the outrage of gender-based injustices—all of which developed into abiding themes in her poetry. "Poetry would offer, as ever, the final refuge. It never let me down. Every time I was flooded over, and drowning, poetry pulled me up onto dry land. I survived."

Nabaneeta had a profound and primal need for poetry, not only as a way to cope, but as a way of forming herself. It was a compulsion that came from deep within: she often spoke of the inner pressure she felt that forced her to write. "How do I know who I am until I have 'written' myself, and read myself? There I was, me, Nabaneeta, taking shape, on a piece of paper." It was critically important for her to write each and every day; a day without a single line of poetry was, for her, "a sad day, a barren day." And yet, shortly after her divorce was finalized, Nabaneeta made a conscious decision to take a step back from her poetry. Why? Because her poems, she felt, were giving her away.

Nabaneeta had always believed that her poems anticipated and understood what she was going through far better than she herself was able to. At that turbulent moment in her life, it felt as if her poetry was, involuntarily yet relentlessly, exposing the rawness of her pain; and in so doing, igniting the readers' obsessive curiosity. "In the case of a woman writer, readers are not content with the literary work alone," she wrote. "They are thirsty for glimpses of her personal life, for extra-literary information."

There was another reason why Nabaneeta took a break from writing poetry for public consumption, and that, too, had everything to do with being a woman writer.

Even when her poems were not inspired by her own life, her readers concluded, rather oppressively, that they were autobiographical. Nabaneeta wrote and spoke extensively about this inescapable "imprisonment" of a woman writer's autonomous identity:

> *A woman writer is constantly watched, like prisoners in a jail who are made to parade before the warden every morning. Her name becomes an essential part of the text that she produces, along with her whole personal life and her body . . . I stopped writing poetry and shifted to humorous prose because my readership had started finding deep personal messages about my private life in my poems, which bothered me. Inevitably, the woman writer's personal life becomes an integral part of her writing, to be analysed and approved by the reader, which is not something the male writer experiences or suffers.*

Therefore, to resist being forced against her will to be "part of the text" in her poetry, Nabaneeta made the radical choice of willingly entering the text in her prose. Throwing open the doors to her "private life," she invited the curious crowd into her household and "let them see it for themselves." She decided to write about herself and her seemingly "dysfunctional" family, which in fact functioned perfectly without any men, in her raucously fun-loving "broken home." Nabaneeta's inimitable prose, which was as truthful as her poems but intensely funny, quickly gained in popularity. Though she could not stay away too long from poetry—"my companion, my fulfilment, my frustration"—a part of her would always regret the great demand that arose for her stories: "I think it harmed me in some way, because as I started writing prose the flow of my poetry decreased."

The truth is, her narrative prose did more closely reflect the public persona of everyone's beloved, ever-optimistic and rambunctious "Nabaneeta Di." Candid yet satirical and observant, her stories, essays, travel writing, children's books and journalism all had a seriousness of purpose and a strong feminist core, but were warm, witty and spry. The vastly popular, as opposed to literary, following she attracted was drawn above all to this category of work, which overflowed with her natural charm and her famous joie de vivre. But if she opened her heart in her prose, Nabaneeta continued to bare her soul in her poetry, without inhibition. It is not easy to distil 60 years of poetry into one slim volume, yet across the years there is a remarkable and obvious consistency in the themes, refrains and tone of her poetry. In contrast to her work in other genres, her poetry is visceral and inward-looking, often painful and sometimes disturbing, but always breathtaking in the power of its truth. Nabaneeta loved to laugh at herself in her prose; but she was never afraid to cry in her poetry.

In fact, Nabaneeta often made the observation that she had grown up with two eyes that were physically "quite un-alike"; one did not know how to smile, and the other could never shed a tear. "I use the smiley-eye to write funny stories. The sad one looks within, and writes poetry." However, even if her two eyes did look and behave as differently as she believed, they were nonetheless "alike" in the candour and boldness of their gaze. Intrepid as ever, Nabaneeta looked long and hard at herself through her work. Her unforgiving honesty rounded into a self-deprecating humour in her prose, that irreverent laughter that was so infectious and loved; equally, it added a sharp edge of anxiety and self-questioning to her poetry, layering it with a depth of palpable sadness.

For Nabaneeta, poetry was a momentous, even sacred, responsibility, a quest for a deeper, more elusive truth, and she held herself accountable for every choice she made as a poet. Even as she embraced poetry as a great blessing in her life, she often noted (only half-jokingly) that she also felt cursed by poetry—it was "like an inevitable curse that had descended upon me at the moment of my birth." Throughout her writing life, her poems revealed a profound recognition of not only the freeing power of words, but also their destructive potential. Whether she described language as a wild stallion or a fiery volcano, as the uncaring aristocracy or a cunning moneylender, as poisonous stings or blood-shedding weapons, we see Nabaneeta grappling with the devastation that can lurk behind language—and even invoking it, in her own words, for "the sake of poetry." More than her prose, it was her poetry that exposed the contours of her own fraught relationship with language, as starkly as it captured her frustrations with the writing process. "Poetry is like war," she wrote. "A war with oneself. Finally, only when there is victory and peace, poetry follows. Poetry has to be earned."

In turn, poetry earned and retained primacy in the creative sensibility of Nabaneeta, who saw herself, in her own words, as "a poet before anything else." Perhaps it was because poetry was "entwined in the very nerve-centres" of her being that it even found ways to insinuate itself into the other genres in which Nabaneeta shone throughout her long career, including her novels and her academic work. While discussing the ways in which her writing reflected her soul and her heart, we must not overlook the brilliant work that came together in her head: Nabaneeta was a widely recognized and exceptionally creative academic, a distinguished professor of comparative literature, whose scholarly work had an extensive focus on poetry.

As a young researcher, first at Harvard and then in Cambridge, Nabaneeta examined the linguistic composition and thematic bases of epic poetry across the world, calibrating the great Indian epics against their counterparts in the Western canon. Her analysis of the verse of the Valmiki Ramayana broke radically new ground, providing evidence of the oral rather than written composition of the epic's early portion (*Balakanda*). Equally pioneering was her feminist study of the retellings of the Ramayana by women poets from the sixteenth century till the present, the subject of her acclaimed Radhakrishnan Memorial Lecture series delivered at Oxford University in 1997. And Nabaneeta's own creative reimaginings of the epics from the perspectives of women, composed in prose as well as poetry, left a blazing trail for younger writers and scholars to follow.

Poetry played a leading role in many of Nabaneeta's novels as well, in form and in content. She revolutionized the fiction form in her bestselling novel *Bama-Bodhini* (*A Woman's Primer*) when she incorporated poems and ballads into its narrative structure, letting the story unfold as much through poetry as through prose. And her novel *Prabashe Daiber Bashe* (*In a Foreign Land, by Chance*) centres on a young Bengali poet who, after emigrating to England, makes a calculated decision to write her poems only in English. Thus, as early as 1977, Nabaneeta had anticipated the global explosion of Indian writing in English, addressing head-on the linguistic and political dilemma of choosing "the language of the ruler" over your own mother tongue.

Nabaneeta was a truly bilingual writer (almost all her academic writing was in English), but as a poet, she consciously eschewed the choice that her novel's protagonist had made. In fact, Nabaneeta's own story was exactly the reverse: when she relocated to Kolkata from London, she resolved to stop writing poems in English, even though she found the unencumbered anonymity, the "cultural distance" and "verbal personality" of English to be liberating. "In English I could express my anger, my thirst, far more openly and powerfully, irrespective of a reader's sentiment, because I was addressing a faceless reading public . . . In English, only the poem exists." Nabaneeta readily acknowledged that English allowed her the freedom to "use language without social-sexual inhibition," which was simply not possible for her in Bengali (one reason, perhaps, why Ma translated so few of her English poems into Bangla). She was also acutely aware of the many advantages, national and international, of choosing to write in English: "In this country mother tongues we have many, father tongue just one. A better control over the father tongue gets you a better deal in the present system of things." And yet, Nabaneeta was unswerving in her election of Bengali as her preferred language for all of her creative writing.

"I wrote in Bangla because it was a political choice for me," she stated without hesitation whenever questioned. She saw this dilemma as a crisis of loyalty, and of identity—not only because she belonged to a generation of writers who rejected the colonizers' language, but even more critically, because she was deeply worried about the future of regional languages and literatures in India. "There is a cultural distance growing between us and our children, who are moving away from their mother tongues." Younger generations across multilingual India were losing their connection to their regional heritages, she warned, owing in part to the dominance of Hindi popular culture, but also to the proliferation of Indian writing in English. Consequently, regional literatures were in danger of seeming increasingly obscure, redundant, or obsolete, she feared. When a journalist asked Nabaneeta why she no longer wrote poetry in English, her unequivocal answer was: "Because I believe it is very important that we write in our regional languages. That way you are serving yourself as a poet, and also serving your language."

Nabaneeta, as voracious a reader as she was prolific a writer, admired and keenly followed new Indian writing in English; at the same time, she recognized the threat that it unwittingly posed. Speaking on "International Poetry, Translation, and Language Justice" at Columbia University in 2017, she drew attention to the scarcity of

English translations from regional languages; as a result, she contended, "Indian literature in English has only naturally raised itself to the status of representing all of India, when only 2% of the nation still read English." Therefore, parallel to her steadfast call to action for writing in the mother tongue, Nabaneeta campaigned hard for translation as "a practical tool for empowerment," one that could, in time, rescue regional literatures from extinction:

> *Good English translations of Indian literature are urgently needed today as lifesavers, to protect regional literatures from being wiped out in the tsunami of globalized Indian literature in English. We need to show the world the features of India's mature inner face, expressed through its many-coloured regional cultures . . . If good translations are available to all, then the world will not have to depend on the Indian writer in English as the only literary interpreter of Indian culture.*

Nabaneeta attributed the three main "discontents of translation" in India to quantity, quality, and availability. There were not enough English translations of regional literatures; most translations did not do justice to the original texts; and our translations were poorly marketed and distributed within and outside India. Consequently, regional literatures were being relegated to a lower literary status: "This false perception has to be met with powerful translations of modern Indian classics," she argued, time and again.

As a language activist as well as a champion of poetry, polyglot Nabaneeta walked the talk to the fullest. A dedicated and dexterous translator, she translated into English the sixteenth-century Ramayana of Chandrabati, the first woman poet who wrote in Bangla (also the first Bengali poet to rewrite Ram's story from Sita's perspective). Nabaneeta's English translation of Chandrabati has been hailed, nationally and internationally, as a radiant and path-breaking presentation of an unrecognized classic.

Nabaneeta was equally passionate about translating poetry into Bangla—a language shared by 250 million worldwide—particularly women's poetry from across India and, indeed, around the world. It was her firm belief that translation could effectively counter the "divisive forces" of "caste, class, religion, gender, region, language," and that it was "especially important to get to know one another in these days of fragmentation and disconnection." Nabaneeta wrote and spoke of translation as a unifying "act of pulling down the fences, of bringing neighbours together," as an empowering tool to "help us realize the falsity of boundaries" and find our "deeper, inner bonds."

Blessed with a formidable gift for languages, Nabaneeta, throughout her career, devoted much of her time to translating poetry from languages as far apart as Kannada or Kashmiri, Gujarati or Malayalam, Chinese or Russian, Japanese or Hebrew. If she didn't know a particular language well enough, she punctiliously used a bridge language, or the help of a collaborator who was fluent in it, until she was satisfied with the truth of her translation. Even when she was severely ill, Ma pored over the proofs of *Shara Prithibir Kabita* (*Poems from the Whole World*), her last book of translations, published a few weeks after she died.

My mother's lifelong commitment to translating women's poetry brings us back full circle to where we started: her unshakeable faith in poetry as an instrument for women's freedom and unity. Speaking at a conference of South Asian Women Writers, she identified women's poetry as the platform "where all languages meet and melt into one another" to give voice to "the shared memories, the shared apprehensions, the shared metaphors," representing a collective quest to "be empowered by the Word, to be freed by the Word." But for Nabaneeta, in addition to being a "precious bond that joins us in sisterhood," poetry embodied a mighty matrilineal legacy to be passed down from generation to generation.

Nabaneeta was born, we know, into a home replete with poetry. She owed her love of languages, as well as her expertise in poetic forms and structure, to her erudite and soft-spoken father, the poet Narendra Dev. But it was her uncompromising mother, Radharani Debi, with whom she shared an intimate if intricate relationship, who showed Nabaneeta the transformative power of poetry. Married at 12 and widowed at 13, Radharani educated herself entirely on her own, remarried (quite scandalously at the time), and became a bestselling poet who wrote under two distinct identities (with two very differently "feminine" poetic personalities). Till her last years, my grandmother remained Ma's most devoted reader, her most scrupulous editor, and her strongest literary critic. Nabaneeta proudly acknowledged, time and again, that she had inherited her profound faith in poetry from her mother:

> *Looking at Bengali women's poetry from Chandrabati to Radharani to myself, we have seen marginal women craftily moving centre stage through poetry. We see that poetry can become a powerful weapon in the hand of the disempowered and can elevate their lives. I am grateful to my mother's poetry, which opened the door for me to walk through.*

I am not a poet, though my mother had wished, not too secretly, that I would become one. But I, too, am grateful to my mother's poetry, which opened the door for me to walk through—as a woman, a mother, a writer, an actor, an activist. Our mother's poetry has always been a tremendous source of strength for me and my sister, just as her own mother's was for Ma.

When I left home early to study, Ma and I stayed connected through her poetry (apart from the six or nine minute "trunk calls" between Kolkata and Boston every Saturday morning, calculated then by increments of three minutes). Though this was long before the magic of email, Ma, always a passionate letter-writer, found generous ways to share her poems with me. Blue aerogrammes and yellow envelopes regularly arrived from India, usually filled with lengthy remonstrations, but sometimes, with poetry. Whenever she sensed a sadness in me, or if ever there was a special reason to celebrate, lines of poetry arrived by post a few days later—sometimes quiet and wise, sometimes silly and joyful, but always comforting. Clippings or photocopies of her published poems were often lovingly folded into the heart of her letter.

In truth, *Acrobat* had its beginnings well over 30 years ago, when Ma and I first started translating her poems together. This was born purely out of need—I wasn't focused on translation at that time. But Ma was often invited to give poetry readings while on a lecture tour, and had little of it available in translation. On such an occasion, when I was a Freshman at Harvard, she was requested by the Bunting Institute to present and discuss her poetry in a special session for the Radcliffe Fellows—and we had to quickly get to work. It was ironic of course that, while Ma was deeply committed to translating the work of women poets across the globe, she translated her own only under duress. We spent a good part of my Sophomore spring break working on translations too, when I visited my mother at Colorado College, where she held the Maytag Chair of Creative Writing and Comparative Literature. I cherished that time we spent together working through and arguing over her poetry, a time that came to an abrupt and heartbreaking end when my grandmother had a stroke, and Ma returned to Kolkata.

Despite her untiring advocacy for translation, my mother continued to resist translating her own poems, a reluctance I found especially frustrating because whenever she did it, her own translations were truly beautiful— and far superior to any done by others. But Ma never hid the fact that she lacked the patience and indeed the motivation to translate her own poetry. As a perfectionist, she agonized over every syllable of every poem she wrote in Bangla, but once she completed a poem, she felt her work was done. "I would rather write a new poem," she would say, than revisit one through translation.

So, our translations were always sparked by practical necessity: Ma needed to have strong translations of her poetry available for her own use. I did not aspire to become the primary translator of Ma's poetry, nor was it important to me to be credited for the work we had done together. In 2012, while we were on a trip to China, Ma had an opportunity to present her poetry in Beijing's Bookworm bookstore, and I was asked to be "in conversation" with her. As she had a book of new poems out (*Tumi Monosthir Koro*), we were keen to include those in the discussion and I quickly translated just a few for the reading, translations that Ma really liked. So, on my mother's 75th birthday the next year, I presented her with *Make Up Your Mind*, a bilingual edition of my translations from her book. (It was a self-published print run of only 75 copies, which was subsequently reprinted several times in much larger quantities.) Because this project was planned as a birthday surprise, I did not involve Ma in the translations at all; she told me afterwards that she was delighted that I hadn't. It had "freed" me, she said, to make my own interpretations and trust my instincts, while staying true to the words, images, and rhymes on the page. And that, in essence, is what I've tried to do in *Acrobat*.

As we know, poetry is never easy to translate, even less so if the poet favours complex rhyming and rhythmic structures, and repetitions that are sublimely melodious or pointedly dissonant. My mother, who called herself "furiously obverse" in her poetic diction, also had an extraordinary talent for creating new words, powerful neologisms that fit perfectly and indispensably into a poem, but were nigh impossible to translate. In addition, even as her images sparkled with piercing originality, they often caressed her own cultural history with a tender specificity (and at times, dissension). And if conveying all of that in English wasn't demanding enough, Ma loved using words that had multiple meanings and resonances, forcing a translator to make some very difficult choices.

Underlying it all, trembled the delicate question of cultural and linguistic loyalty, so central to my mother's poetic sensibility. Some of her more raw, more hurt poems required an especially fine balance to ensure they did not lose their intimacies and nuanced vulnerabilities when translated into English. Perhaps this dilemma was best described by the Sanskritist Barbara Stoler Miller, a close friend of Ma's who was the first to translate one of her Bangla poems into English, in the seventies. Stoler Miller had observed at the time that negotiating between the two languages was bound to be a fraught process: translating her friend's work "demanded more than the usual scholarship of words, images, concepts, poetic traditions, and historical contexts" because it intimately involved her in the risks that Ma had taken in exposing her "imaginations and verbal energies to the censure of the father tongue."

As I wrestled with the particular challenges of translating my mother's poetry, I was often guided by a line of questioning that she had raised herself, as a translator, in her essay "Translating Between Cultures: Translation and Its Discontents." She had laid out in it several fundamental questions to help translators set guidelines for themselves. Do you prioritize the matter or the spirit of the piece? Do you keep your translation literally faithful or opt for a freer rendering? How do you transmit an author's unconventional syntactical and grammatical usage into another language? How do you deal with cultural and linguistic details like rituals and gestures, or colloquialisms and idioms? Do you explain references to history and literature? Do you retain the meter and rhyme of the original, and if so, at what cost? What about line breaks and stanza divisions?

Like any other translator, I wanted the translations to be effortless in their flow, to not "read like translations." At the same time, I had resolved to be faithful to each poem in as many ways as I could be, in content as well as in form, and without the help of footnotes. Sometimes that meant choosing linguistic and cultural equivalents over a more literal "fidelity," and very often it necessitated having faith in the reader's awareness and sensitivity. A question I often asked myself was, how would Ma have written this poem in English, delivering all the nuances of thought, feeling and cadence she achieved in Bangla? In the process of forming an answer to that question, many of my renditions grew closer to English adaptations rather than clear-cut translations. And in making this choice, I was emboldened by Ma's wholehearted endorsement of my earlier renderings of her poems, such as "Alphabet Bird," in which I had added several lines (including "I cage language"), and introduced a few more rhymes than in her original.

Ma loved rhymes, which she used masterfully to create meaning, underscore emotions, and craft revelations. She often generously noted, in articles and interviews, how pleased she was that my translations stayed true not only to her verbal and emotional nuances but preserved her rhyming and metrical patterns, which apparently none of her other translations had tried to do, including her own. Taking her nod as a cue, I made it a priority that in *Acrobat* any poem that Ma had written in rhyme be rendered in rhyme, retaining a similar metrical scheme whenever I could. I also followed, as much as possible, the line breaks and stanza divisions in the original, so that the poem "looked" the same on the page, though this was at times particularly difficult, given the linguistic structure of Bengali. As Carolyne Wright, who had methodically collaborated with Ma (and other Bangla speakers, including myself) on co-translating her poetry, rightly pointed out, "In comparison with English, Bengali is a very dense, concise language. One inevitable result is that a 'narrow' short-lined poem in Bengali becomes a 'fat' long-lined English poem."

Most of the poems in *Acrobat* do reflect the rhyme, rhythm, and shape of the original, negotiated through multiple rounds of compulsive rewriting to achieve a balance between the competing demands of form and of content. In this respect I am truly my mother's daughter. I don't have her multifaceted virtuosity, but I did inherit what my "very finicky" mother called her "terrible habit of writing and rewriting and re-rewriting every single piece." Ma was brutally honest about her writing "neuroses," her obsessive apprehensions as a poet, all of which I can proudly say I have inherited. As she often confessed:

> *I can never meet a deadline. I keep on changing my manuscript even while correcting my proofs, until the press is in tears . . . Every time a poem comes out, I feel it needed a lot more work . . . Every word matters. Every punctuation matters. It is a question of life and death.*

I do exemplify every exasperating trait that my mother owns up to here, as the brilliant team at Archipelago Books, to whose infinite patience I owe a great debt of gratitude, would attest. But this bequest of perfectionism is not the only reason why it has taken me more than a year to complete this book.

In this year, I've used my mother's poetry to keep her close. I've held on to each poem like it was a letter from Ma to me. Her words made me feel as if she was right by my side—I could hear her voice, wrapping her words in all its deep Bengali beauty. I've spent months over every poem, excruciating over each word, revising each punctuation mark. Looking back, I see all the ways in which I've resisted completing this book, as clearly as I see that it's time, now, to let go. It is time to share her poet's voice, hoarse and silken, with all of you.

Here, then, is Nabaneeta's "charmed amulet" or "magic armour," the poetry that roamed "the solitary corners" of her existence: "Every word written is a lifelong quest for that ultimate poem. Will I be able to write the poem? The lines that will live on after me?"

—Nandana Dev Sen

Sources

Chandrabati's Ramayana, Translated from Bengali by Nabaneeta Dev Sen. Zubaan Books, 2020

Panel on "International Poetry, Translation and Language Justice." Institute for Comparative Literature and Society, Columbia University, September 23, 2017

"My Magical Journey through Comparative Literature," Keynote Address by Nabaneeta Dev Sen. Centre for Comparative Literature, Visva-Bharati University, March 6, 2017

"Mother, Daughter, and Words," Interview of Nabaneeta Dev Sen and Nandana Dev Sen on translation. *The Telegraph*, August 27, 2016

"Nabaneeta and Nandana: They travel the world, read poetry and dance the night together," Interview of Nabaneeta Dev Sen and Nandana Dev Sen. *The Telegraph*, April 16, 2016

"Translation and Multilingualism," Sujit Mukherjee Memorial Inaugural Lecture by Nabaneeta Dev Sen. University of Hyderabad, February 11, 2014

"Translating Between Cultures: Translation and Its Discontents" by Nabaneeta Dev Sen. India–Bangladesh Festival of Books and Writers, Dhaka, November 2, 2007

"Writing in a Time of Siege: The Role of Poetry and Literature in Implementing Pluralistic Democracy" by Nabaneeta Dev Sen. Chicago University, November 12, 2005

"First Confidence: My Life, My Work" by Nabaneeta Dev Sen. Sahitya Akademi, New Delhi, August 12, 2004

Interview of Nabaneeta Dev Sen by Ritu Menon. *Storylines: Conversations with Women Writers,* Women's World and Asmita Resource Centre for Women, 2003

"Shared Metaphors, Shared Dreams: Women Writers of South Asia," President's Address by Nabaneeta Dev Sen. SAARC Writers' Conference, 2000

"The Wind Beneath My Wings" by Nabaneeta Dev Sen. *Indian Journal of Gender Studies, Vol. 6, No. 3,* Sage Publications, 1999

"The Hero and His Clay Feet: When Women Retell the Ramayana," Radhakrishnan Memorial Lectures by Nabaneeta Dev Sen. Oxford University and All Souls College, 1997

"Who Is the Mother of These Words? Women, Poetry and Freedom" by Nabaneeta Dev Sen. Kavi Bharati, November 16, 1996

"Poets and Revolutionaries," Interview of Nabaneeta Dev Sen by Elisabeth Bumiller. *May You Be the Mother of a Hundred Sons: A Journey Among the Women of India*, Random House, 1990

"A Choice of Fidelities: Translating Bengali Women Poets" by Carolyne Wright. *New England Review and Bread Loaf Quarterly, Vol. 11, No. 4*, 1989

"Eroticism and the Woman Writer in Bengali Culture" by Nabaneeta Dev Sen. International Seminar on Eroticism in Literature, University of Toronto, 1987

"Splitting the Mother Tongue: Bengali and Spanish Poems in English Translations" by Barbara Stoler Miller, Nabaneeta Dev Sen and Agueda Pizarro de Rayo. *Signs, Vol. 3, No. 3*, University of Chicago Press, 1978

Acrobat

The Unseen Pendulum

Acrobat

She thought she knew acrobatics rather well.
That she could juggle time with both hands,
Play with the now, right next to the then,
She would make both dance, she thought, fist to fist—
And she would glide, so smooth, along the tightrope,
She thought she could do absolutely anything at all.

Only once in your life will the rope shiver.

Memories of a Floral Clock

standing still by the nameless road
I hear the violence of rain
beating on the panes
going dark

switching off the engine is not
switching off memory
your eyes
the floral clock
survive the rain
and your tongue
the unseen pendulum
keeps ticking away
deep inside me
telling time
under the soil

Composed in English by the poet

The Lamp

(Memories on my mother's birthday)

"Go to sleep now, Ma,
It's way past eleven."
"Eleven? It's still early, then!
But *you* must go to bed,
you're teaching tomorrow."

Ma sits in her easy chair,
thick glasses perched on her thin nose,
pale fingers clutching her magnifying glass,
The Statesman spread out across her lap.
Next to her, on the table, her flask of tea, her medicines,
her fragrant betel-leaf in its silver case,
her brass spittoon, her cash-box.
Behind her, on the teapoy, an earthen vase
filled with her favourite white tuberoses,
and a wicker table lamp, woven in Agartala.
Before her, the alarm clock ticking away,
her travelling timepiece.

As Ma turns the pages of the newspaper,
its noisy crackle splinters the quiet night.

Closing my book, I come to her.
As soon as I step inside, I drown
in the deep perfume of those tuberoses.
The nurse is dozing in her chair.
"Ma, please go to sleep now.
It's one-thirty."
"One-thirty?" She scolds. "And you're still awake?
Don't you have college tomorrow?"
Swallowing the rebuke, I keep on wheedling.
"You'll get sick, Ma, if you stay up like this.
You must take care of your body ..."
"My body?" Ma breaks into laughter that sparkles,
like jewellery shimmering from head to toe.
"How much more sick can it get?
And what use is my body, anyway?"

I go to her one more time, before I sleep.
"It's two-thirty, Ma, do call it a night.
Come, let me take you to your bed."
"Yes I'm coming, just coming,
there's only this one tiny bit left.
Reading isn't so easy now, you see—
it's the gift of these cataracts!"
With a slight smile, embarrassed, apologetic,
she buries herself again in printed words.

Under the glowing light of the table lamp,
with her focus on the magnifying glass,
the ticking of the alarm clock
fades away.
As I walk back to my room,
I hear her speaking softly to the nurse.
"No, no, my dear,
don't turn off the light.
Keep that lamp switched on, please.
I have just one more page left ..."

Just one more page left
one more paragraph, one more sentence—
give me one more word, dear nurse,
just one more day.

Poem on My Birthday

In one eye hangs half a teardrop,
In the other, nothing.
Is the girl sleeping? Or is she awake
But lost in dreams? In thought?

The girl is asleep.
Left arm flung across her forehead,
Right hand on her lips.
If this silent household awakens,
The girl will not wake up.
In her one eye sways a teardrop,
In the other, nothing.
All day, all night,
Her ears ring with wild applause
Like a waterfall in the monsoon.
The girl remains asleep, a tear in one eye,
In the other, nothing.

Long ago, the girl had seen a trapeze act
In a circus. Two acrobats were flying
Like birds, from perch to perch.
All around them, a great emptiness,
And in the centre, long swings,

Swaying in celebration—
Awake or asleep, night or day,
The girl is lost in a dream of trapeze.
In one eye swings a teardrop,
In the other, nothing.

Sound: One

When you say, "Love me a lot!"
And call out, both arms swaying,
Somewhere, in an abandoned plot,
A wedding band starts playing
And the train crosses the bridge.

Sound: Two

Like an old alarm clock
You start ringing in my heart
I shut my ears tight

The Last Gust

Spreading out upon the floor
we warm our limbs
under Red Cross blankets
huddled up against bodies
unfamiliar but warmth-giving
we shiver in the hailstorm
like stray kittens

we dream of rippling yellow
paddy fields, the lake mirroring
brass pitchers, made golden
on narrow waists and proud heads
by an admiring sun
cringing, we hide our scars
under strange pubic hair

we dream of laughing brown faces
thrown skywards
in careless abandon
baring white ivory
upon polished mahogany

clinging to unfamiliar bodies
under donated blankets
we wait
for the last gust of wind
to snatch
the thatched roof
away

Composed in English by the poet

Change

Everyone changes little by little
never completely, not all the way—
but only a little, just enough to transform
summer, monsoon, winter, night and day.

Shame

Why should you be ashamed if
Spring tells the same lie for years?
Why be ashamed of your tears?

The Emperor's New Clothes

the maple lets its red-gold regalia slip down
and gather around its ankle
unrobed, it stands
in a constant state of erection
feeling imperious
until
a robin arrives
and flies away, teasing

then spring rushes in
with its age-old clothes
and covers up
his ludicrous highness

Composed in English by the poet

The Shell

Stepping upon my past
A warm chestnut shell just emptied
I hear it crackle under my feet
Crisply into the dust

Its echo rattles down the street
Towards a childhood mist

Composed in English by the poet

The Great Fair

You would take me to the Great Fair,
You had promised.
I'd buy a bamboo flute,
Splashed with colours.
A small chariot, two clay horses,
Little pots and pans, toys, a mask,
A golden-haired, glass-eyed doll.

Making a list long enough
To buy up the whole fair,
Filling my little cup
With all the coins I'd saved,
I waited for you on my steps—
You were going to come back
And take me with you
To the Great Fair.

As I waited on my steps
My limbs grew long
My list blew away in the wind
My cup of change became a trunk of gold.

There is nothing left for me to buy
From your Great Fair anymore.

I am going to get up from my steps now

This Child

One day this child too will die.

This child, pure as milk, whom I've brought into this world
with all my heart's desire, and with fervent prayer.
If she asks me now, "On what promise
have you thrust me into this strange and dazzling world?
What grand celebration must I attend?"
I will be petrified.
Choking with fear, with ignorance,
I will run away
to a dark cave, numb and empty.

What answer will I give you?

The Yellow River

the great wall of china
rises within
blocking all
the stars the woods the rice fields

the great wall of china rises inside
besieging centuries
blocking all

yet
the yellow river
sweeps away village
after village

Translated by the poet

All those crazy blue hills

All the blue hills slowly fade away
behind the advancing wall of cloud,
and suddenly
a naked tree rises in front
with implausible clarity.
An errant ray of the hidden sun
embellishes it abruptly,
almost ludicrous.
Its gnarled hands get tangled up, as if
the curtain-ripping light startles it
while it's secretly immersed in private affairs.
The tree
looks mighty, many-armed, and fierce,
like the copper statue of a nude god.
As the ornate backdrop gets steadily lost
under thick layers of white,
every white wave is fringed with pure gold
along the slope of every hill.
The tall tower captures in its grasp
all that there is to hold.
As if a fire has broken out inside the summit's window,
a sliver of flame dances around the pointed peak,
like a falling angel encircled by light.

And
under reddish roofs, all those white houses
suddenly grow inward, languid, weary.
Then
the clouds change their music, then
the lights change their dance, and then
all the blue hills are born again
from empty space.

Flute

It was the wrong moment
to stop playing your flute.
When you turn around now,
what do you expect to see?
The figure that was following you
all this while, so softly, step by step,
returned to the world of shadows,
forever.

Friend

You keep calling for your memory,
but forgetting comes without a call.
Seat both down next to you, because
forgetting could be a friend after all—
when memory becomes your enemy.

Time

She is only asking for time
Five minutes, nothing more.
Because she knows
She can easily stretch
Those five minutes
Into a lifetime.

I Cage Language

In Poetry

Stay alive
Show yourself clearly
Like the unfailing passport photo
Stay awake in every line, you,
Like an unquenchable thirst
Yes, you,
The pain that tears my heart apart,
Show yourself clearly
Like a flower in full bloom
Don't hide from me

As long as I live in poetry

Alphabet Bird

When night falls
I search for him
I bring him home
I look him in the eye
And I cage
Language

When day breaks
Once again the world
Wraps around my eyes
And off he flies
Taking each word
That alphabet bird

Heartbeat

The meaning of the word "heartbeat"
changed for her suddenly that day.
Just as the tiny bluebell bursts through deep snow
for the first time, all alone, so brave.
Just as the sliver of light falls on one side of the face,
glowing like a fond memory.

Words are flighty. Like fortune's goddess,
they flit from home to home,
changing their character, and their heart.
The face of the word "heartbeat" suddenly hardened,
like a cunning moneylender appearing at the door,
clutching the deed of debts accrued since birth.
And so, signing the bond for her lifetime,
this free woman became a slave to one word:
"heartbeat."

The Lie

I asked them,
"Whose are you,
Dear Mirror, Flower, Desire?"
They replied,
"Why, we are yours, of course."
I said, "Never."
They smiled.

I asked again,
"Whose are you,
Mirror? Flower? Desire?"
They replied,
"Yours, only yours."
I said, "I don't believe you."
They wept.

The day I called out,
"Mirror, you are mine.
Flower, you are mine.
Desire, you are mine."
That day
The silver storm roared out in anger,
"That's a lie!"

I said, "No, no . . ."
The storm shouted,
"A lie!"
I cried, "You're mine, mine!"
None of them replied.

The silver storm crackled in laughter, echoing,
"Liar."

Broken Home

Once again you glow, on the brink of love
Once again you're dazzling in heartbreak
Is it for the sake of poetry, then, that
Once again you're hunting for pain?

Do you break your home just for poetry,
Time and again?

That Word

You've been waiting to hear
that word for a lifetime.
Now at last, that word rings
right inside your ear—
like a storm of bee wings
from a broken hive.

Night and day, a buzzing curse,
violently alive.
And then that word, so loud,
is turned into a falsehood
by the roar of the cloud,
as it pierces the universe.

Four letters? Six? Or is it five?
Which tongue? For whose good?
Who built the nest?
Bees swarm from the broken hive
without rest.
Do you hear their angry wings?
Stings, poison, honey, poison, stings.

A Birthday Voodoo

(For Ruth Feldman)

I am reading your poems, Ruth,
and thinking of relationships
between speechless animals
and grains of rice
between stars and planets
the sea and water
between us

I am thinking about relationships
between yesterdays and tomorrows
the magical relationship
between space and time

Can't blame those memory cells
how much can they bear
how much can they cheat and wipe out
Witness Cheat Witness Cheat Witness

The magic of time
sometimes works only in one direction
like turning black into grey
but sometimes it also flows against the current
and shatters the unshatterable—
such is the voodoo of time

Otherwise, on this warm afternoon
in the sweltering heat of Calcutta
reading your poems about the snow-drizzling Boston sky
why should I think of time—
tail in mouth, mouth in tail,
unbroken, unbreakable

I can see you, Ruth, at your computer
playing with Primo, your old friend,
translating his pain
those burning furnaces
those beautiful lampshades made of fine skin
those fashion wigs of human hair
I can smell the fumes
and I see it all turning gently, ever so gently, into English
as all those cloistered children
grow up into overexposed adults

From a faraway corner of this planet, the same one,
I am watching it all Ruth,
I am watching it all as I run,
the running away never ends

Happy birthday, Ruth, woman of the riverbank,
I give you this glass window
and this open balcony
with the saffron river next to it, and all the boats
with their naked bright sails,
and naked dark sailors rowing
I give you the steamer's midnight whistle on the Ganga—
the very same that you heard as a young girl
on the Mississippi

I give you this old, old banyan tree by the river,
a wise Rastafarian, with all its roots
hanging from the branches like dreadlocks,
I give you the strong wind, and this strong current,
let it all flow through your joined hands

Happy birthday, Ruth, I can see you
with your easel and your paintbrushes
against the red-gold autumn sky . . .
Keep the empowering memories
and the dreams that follow,
keep Algiers and Siracusa,
keep the Himalayas and the Taj Mahal
I want to wrench from you
Buchenwald

Composed in English, on Ruth Feldman's 85th birthday

Poetry Witch

She came, yes,
that demoness came back,
cutting through all three ages.
Taking a long, long sip
from my bare vein, she said—
Here I am, right beside you,
I am here for you,
I haven't abandoned you yet.
Don't you see?
The smell of blood
draws me back even today.

Combustion

As powerful
As that volcano range
Is this range of alphabets
Touch it
And you'll burn to ashes
Instantly

Take Back the Night

Man: In the twilight, I could still hear the lark
Woman: The night was moonless, oppressively dark

Man: In the flowering woods, a night fairy walked
Woman: In the Sundarbans the man-eater stalked

Man: In that fragrant springtime air
Woman: Blood-drenched remains lay there

Growing-up Lesson

Boy, are you scared of bloodshed?
Are you terrified of plucking virginity?
If the taste of blood goes to your head,
Do you fear that it will be a calamity?
The truth is, whether wrong or right,
Your blood calls out to you each night.

Listen, boy, it's time for you to grow.
Words can be as fierce, don't you know?
The treachery that lingers on tongue tips—
Beyond the world that all your dreams show,
Know that blood can be easily shed by lips.

The Ocean

Once again, the ocean speaks the truth. Its call
awakens me and I answer it, time after time.
I am not addicted to dreams—no, not at all.
My reality is the ocean's wave-swept rhyme.

Telephone

Sometimes, when I'm busy at home,
I think I hear a ringing upstairs.
It's the telephone. As I drop my work in a rush,
it occurs to me that it can't be ringing here.
We have friends, yes, but we don't have a phone.
Listening carefully, I realize that, in fact,
the phone had never rung. Not in this house,
not in any house. It was just my mistake.
I pick up my work again. As soon as I begin,
the phone starts ringing, far away.
I grow impatient as I wait,
but I hear no one answer the call.
The phone keeps ringing, non-stop.
Though I know it's not in this house.
Nor in that house. Not in any house at all.

A sad song about words

They refuse to be at your beck and call.
Like God's grace,
they need an auspicious moment,
the right mood, or at least a whim.

Words stand aloof
like the false modesty, many-hued,
of a setting sun that leans against the sky—
unattached, unreachable, alone,
yet gently touching the earth's tamed mane
with caressing fingers.

Like the framed image of a perfect couple
lighting up the storefront of a photo studio—
a staged scene between two strangers
who don't remember each other's faces
but are bound by a pose, and by cash,
models of a charmed moment.

So too, words linger, and dazzle
the waiting peaks of your brain
like the pink rays of a fading sun.
If you lock eyes, there may be
an instant's celebration, but that's all.
Don't think for a moment
that words will ever melt the ice,
or warm you enough to draw you close.
No, never.

Like landed gentry, flawlessly attired,
words step gingerly into
the grand carriage of your imagination,
avoiding the muddy pavement
of your pen.

The Year's First Poem

Pretending
as if nothing at all has happened,
picking up the heart
from the sand, dusting it clean
pushing it back inside my blouse
secretly, the year's first poem gets written.

Won't you kiss me now?
I followed every instruction
of my brain.

Unspoken

Each time you say,
"Forever, forever,"
I only hear,
"Today, today!"

Being

Piecing together
many small lies
a great big truth
takes shape

That truth crushes
all other truths
into a lie

That lie is now
Life

Sapling of a Heart

Be Quiet

Hush, hush, my noisy heart,
Be quiet, don't be a curse!
Thanks to your deafening row,
Heaven, earth, hell
Will wake up now.

Stop, stop this rush in my veins—
If I let my blood gush like the rains
It will flush away the whole universe.

The Jungle Story

my exile is over, mother,
no more living in the jungle for me
come, mother, underneath this matted beard
feel the familiar cheeks of your child
open up your breasts, mother, and watch how
the seven streams of milk
gush towards my parched tongue

look at these feet, mother, the tiny feet
where your golden bells had jingled
look at this arm
upon which you had tied your talisman
when I was born
now look at this chest where you had planted
the sapling of a heart
in a soft green stretch of sun
in the hidden mesh of this dark jungle,
impenetrable,
has grown a hungry tree ...
with toothy leaves and sharp claws
and fierce flowers

it chews on other hearts
a fine flesh-eater

my time in the jungle is over, mother,
now the jungle lives in me.

Translated by the poet

Childspeak

Whenever I see you
That exiled, homeless, street-child within me
Starved for days
Makes a great clamour
Millions of lice under her matted hair
Blood oozing from her chapped skin
Her cries scare the neighbourhood crows away

Every time she sees you
Every time she sees you

That naked street-child starving within me
Abandons her games in the dust
And stretching out her arms against the wind
Wails in hunger:
"Give me love!"

At this, her playmates,
The crows and the street-dogs
Stop their games of snatch and tag
And stand still for two minutes
Upon the garbage heap

Translated by the poet

That Girl

Sorrow had chased her.
The girl kept running and running,
What else could she do?
She hurled the comb in her hand
At sorrow—
And instantly, from the comb's hundred teeth
Sprouted thousands of trees,
A deep forest swarming with wild animals.
And somewhere among the growls of tigers,
In that haunted darkness,
Sorrow got lost.

Fear had chased her.
The girl kept running and running,
What could she do?
She threw her tiny bottle of perfume
At fear—
And instantly, the perfume swelled
Into a foaming, whirling cyclone.
With a deafening roar,
The fierce saffron tide flooded mile after mile,
Sweeping away fear.

The day love chased her
The girl had nothing in her hand.
She kept running and running,
What could she do?
She gouged her heart out from her breast
And flung it at love—
And instantly, that fistful of heart
Sprang up into a range of green mountains,
With cascades and caves, canyons and crests,
Mystery reverberating
In its gorges and its valleys.

The shivering echo
Of stormy winds, the rush of waterfalls,
Its slopes full of shade, and its peak,
Burnt by the sun and the moon.
Perhaps it was
That dazzling, brimful heart
That didn't allow
Her lover's timid love
To advance and grow.

She is chased now by exhaustion.
Empty-handed, empty-hearted,
She keeps running and running,
What can she do?
The girl tosses behind her
Only a sigh—
And instantly
The flame of her breath
Sets fire to her entire past,
Spreading in every direction
A desert of burning, churning sands.

Now the girl runs without a care,
Both arms held high above her head—
At last
She is chased
Only by her destination.

Grief: Rainy-Day Rhymes

These rhymes for you, in this rain,
Are penned in letters of my pain

Where are you, who are so dear?
Some far away, some very near

For some of you, in my mind,
Bells start ringing every time

For some of you, in my heart,
Day and night get torn apart

You were with me just yesterday
Now all of you have gone away

Without you, on this day of rain
All feels empty, and in vain

Story of a Dry Leaf

The other day, on the road,
you had brushed away
a bit of dry leaf
from my hair.

Now I am buried
in a heap of dry leaves,
invisible

Where did you go?

These Beloved Faces

I can no longer bear to watch
my loved ones wilt with age

With my eyes wide open, I can't bear to see
these beloved faces melt like clouds,
as pond scum thickens around the pools of their eyes
the brows collapse like a dead bird's wings,
the lips dry up in the dust
like unripe fruit plucked by storms.
How everything dries,
how everything flies away in the wind
like scraps of paper,
how everything disappears

How the heart folds up its tent
and steps into the road, readying itself
to raise a hand and hail a car for hire
to raise that hand to say goodbye, and go.
The heart retreats and folds, as I now see,
it takes all shining pots and pans from the rack
and shatters them on cold stone with a deafening crash.

How, in the heat of the sun, all sounds fade away,
all traces vanish.
Those beloved faces, like clouds,
change their form and float away

With my eyes wide open, I can't bear to see
The burnt grass in the yard
So close to me

A house, the colour of pain

The house has become the colour of pain,
I can't return to that house again.
Turn the boat around, wind of my heart,
Blow to a different land, to another part.

Crash

Because I keep crashing
into walls, I have now
come to know them all.

Eyeing an open door
I keep trying to run out—
but it's just another wall.

A Poem for My Lover

Whenever you love me
Even the three grey hairs flying around my face
Forget their insensitivity
And throwing Dr. Freud's list to the winds
Become acknowledged erogenous zones
Whenever you love me

Whenever you love me
This planet turns into a private plane
That one built by the Sultan of Brunei
Remember? So scandalously lavish?
I glide over the heads of poor jealous mortals.
Countless closets suddenly overflow with my possessions,
Putting Imelda Marcos to shame
Whenever you love me

Whenever you love me
God takes a quick look at us and wonders:
"Where on earth did these two materialize from?
Did I mess up? Could I have created these
Happy things?" He rubs his eyes in disbelief.
Disbelief? Or envy?
Whenever you love me, even God . . .
Yes
Whenever

Translated by the poet

Too Much

Did I ask for too much, then?
I wanted just two eyes, nothing more.
No dawn, no dusk, no long night—
not food, nor clothes, nor shelter.
Neither remembrance nor reflection,
but a moment's attention, to be erased
in the next moment—that's all.
Still, did I ask for too much?

Out of Reach

You asked for a nameless love, out of reach,
I weaved you a wreath of blooms, each to each.
You want love's temperate breeze, softly sighing,
I blow you a dark thunderstorm, terrifying.
Your love is detached, afar, chaste to its core,
My love is, in part, love—and, in part, war.

A Night Drink

Drinking water in the dark
From a bowl of pickled chillies
The thirst is quenched
But the lips keep burning

Composed in English by the poet

Poison

The full moon collapsed into
the poison pool, murky and black.
How did such venom gather
in my embroidered pillow—
silken, yet ready to attack?

Sparrow, Again

Don't ask me again to be a fairy.
I can't be a fairy any more, at any hour.
Moonlight is frightening,
Loneliness an unbearable weight.
Listen, please—
There's no moonshine left in my heart,
My mind is tightly bound in sunlight.
Let me
be
a sparrow.

Face to Face

There are one or two faces
whose eyes I can't bear to meet.
When I stand before them, I feel
I forgot to brush my teeth,
or wipe away the traces
of dirt from my cheek.

Because some loving faces
shine just like a mirror,
I can see me in them vividly—
closer than even myself,
and clearer.

The Twittering Machine

I have a picture postcard
Stuck on my kitchen wall

Spreading out slender wire branches
Across a bright blue sky
And setting four tiny wire birds upon them
Mr. Paul Klee has created a funny little machine
With a great big lever attached to it, as if
The moment you turn it on
The tiny wire birds will start twittering
Wielding their thin wire tongues
He has called it
The Twittering Machine

Whenever I see that picture I think of you
Four little wire birds
Are hidden within your tiny body
And the lever is held in your small fist
Before you can start talking
You have become a chatterbox

Our very own little Twittering Machine
The one we have made
You—
Filling the bright blue sky

Composed in English by the poet

Mountain

Whether they say it or not, you feel it.
You feel everything.
Somewhere, there is a mountain—
Beyond the small talk, the big words,
Beyond little sorrows and utter heartbreak,
Beyond it all,
Stands a mountain of laughter, of joy.
On that mountain, I will build a home with you
One day.

Whether they say it or not, you feel it.

The Last Act

There he stands, spanning my heart,
Like a dark, black, moonless sky—
Touching, in his pain, every star,
He leaves his footprint in my eye.

Now that you have come, don't leave,
I beg you, can't we make a pact—
The temple is burning, see it heave,
Stay with me to watch the last act.

Do I Know This Face?

First Confidence

Rain sweeps through my drapes
this monsoon morning, as curtains toss,
every door flies open towards the past.
The dry leaves melt away, soaking wet,
the footprints now lie hidden in moss.

I unfold my face into the rain,
I wrap my body in drenched hair.
Now, lifting my eyes, I stand tall
and, in this free and weightless light,
I say with confidence, for the first time—
I have forgotten all.

Sometimes, Love

It comes when called. Like a pet cockatoo,
it sits on my finger, fluttering.
It sways its neck, fluffs its feathers, swings its crest,
and recites its practised lines, uttering
every pleasing word.
My lily-white bird
repeats to me all that it's been taught and sings best.
Saying just what I want to hear,
it pours honey into my ear.

But behind my back, soon after,
alone, perched on its base,
my lily-white bird
clatters its shiny shackles
as it cackles with laughter,
shedding feathers
in empty space.

Puppet

(To Nandana)

I can't decide, was it a mistake? Or is it better this way?
Twice now, pretending to be a goddess,
I've created humans out of my desire.
Funnily, though, that's where the fake goddess act ends.
After that, you revert to being a woman, as before.
Good and bad, dreams, sorrow—
it's all beyond your will again.
So, the puppet's dance will resume once more, on a string.
Practice makes perfect. Always do your best.

I look into the mirror: do I know this face?
Somewhere it lies hidden, that secret divine will.
Or was it just a momentary spark,
the celestial celebration of an instant,
an act of pity by a humorist in the background—
this cloud-bursting, supernatural light?

Renunciation

If this is called life, the life of youth,
I have no craving at all for this thing.
Mother, take back my dreams, my memories.
Take my poetry, the tendrils of my imagination,
the treasure of seven kings.
Everything you gave me, take it all.
A mother's love, the fondness of a friend,
victory, wonder.
I'll unwrap my pouch and easily throw away
the blood-soaked placenta. Purest gold.
All the dreamless, impoverished people of the world—
let their hearts be filled with my dreams.

If this is called life, the life of youth,
then we have simply been tricked—
by all the advertising.

Green Salad for My Husband

(For Germaine Greer)

I have a shock of green ideas upon my head
Ever so green
Ever so raw
Unwashed
Garden-fresh
With pesticides seeping through

A fine salad for my gourmet husband.

Composed in English by the poet

Reflection

In an empty room
at a lonely table
my reflection in the glass whispers,
"How are you, Nabaneeta?"

In an even softer whisper
the steam from my cup of tea
sends the secret reply

Shadow

So, they all got to know
he was never there
it was just his shadow

Children

Children
whirling like tops inside my brain
leaping clapping shrieking creaking
upon the rusty springs of my nerve-ends

children
each a solitary palm tree
in a desert island
sucking up the subterranean waters
to bear branches of bitter bronze fruit

Composed in English by the poet

Metamorphosis

One morning, just like Gregor Samsa,
your whole world too changed forever.
Did you ever think this could happen,
would happen?
Did you ever imagine that, so easily,
lifelong ties of birth could unravel,
with no resistance?

Look, how light are the hands and feet now,
the ribs have melted into fluffy softness,
the muscles can be torn like fine paper.
Now, even the sharp stab of a dagger
would not draw a single drop of blood.

In the afternoon
the maid will sweep the dead insect
into the rubbish bin.

Conversations, Bellagio Center

I'm fine

Honestly, I'm fine.
If my eyes don't look the way they should,
it's only the light.
If my feet don't fall the way they should,
it's only the shoes.
If you don't see the woman you saw in me,
it's only the season.

I am fine.

Composed in English by the poet

So that

I wish I could change the landscape a little
Just a little, a very tiny bit
Like a big fat chimney protruding
From the delicate rows of alpine cottages
Or a leper begging by the lakefront where
We sip our vino or cappuccino
Just so that we know
Where we are

Composed in English by the poet

Doppelganger

You swing from Dubai to Venice
I cling to the lap of my city
You shift from cricket to tennis
I drift in Ganga's tranquillity

Lifeboat

If you say today
You want to be alone
You want to float away
The sea will rush to your door
With its crashing waves

Not with a boat to keep you safe.

Night

"Come to me, come to me!"
The river calls out to you each night
As you sway over the bridge
All alone

Vision

Erase the image of that face
From your eye
Slice it off, gouge it out
Do it
Even if you go blind
So be it.

Taste: A Diptych

Based on the poetry of Lal Ded, the 14th-century Kashmiri mystic

Craving

It could be bitter or sweet,
poison or honey
but it won't be a waste.
What is your craving?
You will recover that taste
if you keep braving
this journey
until the end of the street.

Crushed

I put all of my heart
in a mortar and pestle
crush it into parts—
and then chew it well.

I keep a cool head
but I cannot tell
am I living, or dead?

Cloud

That girl, she wishes she were a bird.
Today, she thinks she'll be an eagle,
Tomorrow, she wants to be a seagull.

That girl, that girl is very stubborn.
She's determined to spread her wings and fly—
Both on the ocean and high in the sky.

But what should she touch first, water or air?
So she becomes a sea breeze on her quest—
Then, a wave's salty kiss, on the wind's breast.

That girl, that girl is very stubborn.
In the end, she made good on her pledge—
She's that rain cloud, on the northeast edge.

This Face

This face, I do not know this face
This tongue, I do not know this tongue
This body of mine
can contain me
no longer

Make Up Your Mind

Make up your mind
Who do you want
That woman, or me?
Within me breathe
Two people—

Make up your mind
Who do you want
That woman,
Or me?

Sacred Thread

Right Now: Forever

Time has not the power to extinguish me,
Don't think for a moment that I wait upon Time.
Let Time keep on playing his absurd battle game,
Every time he strips me, I rise clothed, without shame;
With the force of prayer, of spells magic and divine,
All that was untimely will turn auspicious, sublime.

In a just war, the rebel stands forever unafraid
For her ally is Eternity, who, divinely arrayed,
Guides her chariot, destroying the enemy line.
Thus, a divisive age will be defeated and spurned—
Though it brings on great wars, it will lose every time;
From all our scriptures, this is the truth I have learned.
Know that I am cherished by an undivided, infinite age:
Time will never have the power to scorch me with its rage.

Antara

(To Antara)

Antara, rising from deep within
primordial waters, like the first sun,
forever new, forever old,
you made me the universe.
History and prehistory
file through me now, hand in hand,
in constant evolution.
Antara, by your blessing I have won
the sacred right to enter, and stand
in these timeless halls of gold,
with my foremothers.

Now, clasping your two tiny hands in mine,
I hold the future in my debt, through your birth.
Antara, in an instant you have filled all time—
By your grace, I am now coeval with the earth.

Translated with the poet

The Doctor

Like a phantom
guarding the hidden treasures of half a century
her two clenched hands hold in their grasp
the unconditional promise of asylum.
After all these years, the knot is loosening.
Released from the ties,
one will pass over to the other side,
leaving the other a prisoner on this.

From the moment of birth,
the auspicious exchange of glances
sealed the bond.
That ever familiar face
grows gradually indistinct.
A light from beyond
flashes upon it, changing its pallor,
as the vortex of pain
spins into a mighty whirlwind, pulling into its twist
fifty years
of anger, sorrow, frantic distraught love.

Will the umbilical cord be cut now, at last?
Has the doctor finally arrived?

The Appointment

We would meet, that was the plan.
With pieces of bridges and towers
Clasped in my hand, my love,
In unbroken time
In infinite space
I would wait for you
Same time—
My youth
Same place—
This earth.

Look
My youth is ready, on time,
This earth, well-prepared.
A magnificent bridge has built itself
From all those fragments,
Locking the river into a long smooth stretch.
The broken bits of towers have joined together,
A monumental pillar now pierces the universe.

We would meet, that was the plan.
Look, my love, I am still here—

Is unbroken time an ever-extending wait?

That Invisible Tower

From my plot of grass, I could see you
stepping onto that stairway of air
I watched you as, step by step,
you climbed up the invisible tower

I watched how, reaching the tower's top,
you brushed your cheeks with golden clouds
and touched the sun's hand, making a promise

And suddenly, I was swept away from the mountain
as if by an avalanche, falling at an unbearable speed,
spiralling down a never-ending void

As I was falling, I watched you—
how delicately you treaded air,
and climbed into the neighbourhood of the sun.

Full Moon Nightscape

And yet, there is no sound inside.
Deep in the heart, no sound arises.
The young man by my side
Points to the road of a previous birth
With the moon splayed out on the asphalt
The young man by my side
Points to the moon of a previous birth
A full moon with all its contours
Yet deep in the heart
An answerless, infinite silence
Freezes like dry ice
As if a colony of unspeaking, unhearing people
Flourishes inside me
And yet, one day there was no respite
From rippling music

Eyes, ageing eyes, take it all in
Following the young man's index finger
Eyes, empty eyes, look on even as
Miles and miles of abandoned moon
Lie humiliated
Without a road
Without a word
Without a previous birth

Translated with the poet

And Yet, Life

You know that human desire
does not last in this world.
Even grief does not linger,
it melts away.
Memories too are fleeting.

Poetry flies away as well,
if you let go of the thread—
it flutters in space like a lost kite.
The poet floats in an infinite void, desolate,
like a spacecraft disconnected from earth,
with no destination.

And yet life persists, somehow or other,
just the way you choose to shape it.
Pampered and well-fed in your lap,
or reckless, crushed under your shoe.
Only life remains, body to body,
in an earthen cup, or a silver glass—
as long as you exist.

In Marriage

Stay close. I'm scared.
It feels as if this moment is not true.
Touch me—
like the closest ones touch the body before cremation.
This hand, take it, my hand.
Hold this hand, as long as you're near me
don't leave it untouched. I'm scared.
It feels as if this moment is not true.
As untrue as our long yesterday,
as untrue as our infinite tomorrow.

Festival

The moment one man comes out on the street, a stone in his hand
Two of us stand up to him with brickbats
The moment a man falls, bloodied,
Bright-eyed we lay down seven more, as bloody
The gentle souls who once rushed to care for the wounded
Now stand at their balconies, cheering
Someone's wife has been taken away in the dead of night?
Come, let's drag all the women from their village, stripped naked, in broad daylight
Some bastard has gouged out a boy's eye?
We'll rip out the eyes of the whole nation.

Now we establish a new Rakhi festival
We've fixed up a wonderful programme for Brothers' Day
With a heavy, spiked iron ball dangling from an invisible chain
We shall beat our breasts
And pierce the three worlds every waking moment
With the soundless cry of the soul
*Ha bhai re, ho bhai re**

---

*The mourning chant of Muharram

Put your ear to the anthill
And you shall hear that cry

Translated by Antara Dev Sen

December 1992

Dishes are being shattered
small utensils that make
a poor man's household.

dishes are being shattered
with a deafening noise
like the demolition of a rich man's mansion
shaking up the neighbours' walls

only glasses are breaking

only glasses are breaking
what's so surprising about it?
what's surprising is this
quaking earth
this bubbling blood
this breathless sky
this demented air

only a poor man's household is being shattered
what's so poor about it?

in a poor man's home
poverty has no name
it melts away
like pain
water to water
air to air

Translated by the poet

There was a time

There was a time I loved you so, black cloud,
that's hard now to forget.
And yet, I can let no one know, for, cloud,
Now you have turned blood-red.

Haunted

There isn't a moment
When I don't think of your face.
Night and day, the turn of seasons,
Death or birth—
Like a ghost you've possessed them all,
Air, water, earth

And sometimes, in between,
I am alive

Healing

My eyes are not facing yours
My body is turned the other way
Let my heart
nurse your aching body
Can you recognize its touch,
even today?

Umbilical Cord

(For my mother)

You are in so much pain.

You're trying to cut the birth-knot
but earth's umbilical cord
keeps you tied in twists,
tangled like
our weak and fearful love.

You're trying hard to be born
into a different, fearless world.
But our restless arms, unshakeable
like the sacred thread,
coil around your neck—
a blood-drenched umbilical cord.

You will not have the power
to leave the womb of this earth
and escape freely
into a newborn breeze.
You will be bound here—
in pain, in love.

Locked

The eyes are saying,
it is time—
the question is,
who will unlock the door?

Chained

What a strange island is this
or is it not an island at all
bound to the mainland
with invisible shackles

blossoms of foam on the shore
or is it not foam at all
but a chain of congealed tears
smothering in every direction
the infinite horizon of memory

this island
is it not an island at all
but an illusion of the sea
floating
for all time
alone

I Give to Baser Life

I am fire and air, my other elements
I give to baser life.

I have no need for earth or water
Just fire, air and space
Wipe out the breasts, the waist, the luring eyes
Wipe out tears and laughter
Take back your earth and water

I will keep my skies

Composed in English by the poet

Catch of the Day

I want to chop it up
slice it into pieces
grind it into a paste
season it
then shut it in the oven.

They didn't win—
the sun, the rain, the earth.
It's still all raw inside
floundering like a catfish
still alive, freshly caught:
my youth

Return of the Dead

Receive me then, Kolkata,
I am your true love, your whole world.
I'm back from the war, an aborted mother,
I have brought the ocean with me instead.
My lap is empty, yes, but my breasts
Are heavy, overflowing with wasted milk,
Look at the fathomless salt water
In my eyes.

Come, then, look at me, see how
Virginity burns on my brow again,
Fiery as the setting sun.
Touch me, for my newborn flesh
Belongs to you now—
Receive me then, Kolkata,
In your waiting arms.
Your loneliness is over at last,
I have returned
Just as you had wanted me to.

Why this stunned silence, then?
This anxious glance, this daze?
Lift your face
Don't shift your eyes
Look at me
Your prayers were heard,
Here I am, returned from the dead—
Yes, it's me, your childhood sweetheart,
Your world of passion, your old flame,
Your very own
Nabaneeta

Translated with the poet

A Letter to Ma

It is true
I was created in you.
It is also true
That you were created for me.
　　　　—Maya Angelou

My first semester in college. You arrived in between your conferences, suitcases and admirers in tow. Refusing abundant offers of hospitality in Cambridge, you shared (and immediately redecorated) the one and a half rooms assigned to my two roommates and me. Every morning, you stood in line in our noisy dormitory to claim your three minutes in the shower. You preferred the modern steel-and-glass shower stalls opposite our room to the quieter, more old-fashioned bathroom down the hall.

You left after a week, just as I was getting used to finding your hip-length hair in my comb, and turning every head in the one-thousand-strong Harvard Union when you swept into dinner with me, gliding in like a queen, like you always did.

A few weeks later, we hit midterm exams. I overslept the first day, found the showers occupied and sprinted to the other bathroom in panic. As I stumbled onto freezing tiles and fiddled with the cranky knob that spurted cold water for red and boiling for blue, something miraculously familiar caught my eye. A crimson dot of velvet on the narrow grey wall. Your well-travelled bindi, carefully transported from your forehead and placed beyond reach of the spray. In a flash I could hear your laugh and smell your scent. I could feel the tension in my neck melt into the mist surrounding me. That perfect circle of red gave evidence, on the mildewed wall, that you would always be there. Far away, so close.

Eternity. Poême. J'Adore. Trésor. Happy. Forever and Ever. Why did your favourite perfumes always seem to talk about you? And yet, no matter which one you wore, you always smelled, wondrously, the same. It's that essence of Ma, that adjective-defying, all too familiar fragrance that lingered in your sari before it was washed, that seeped out of your suitcase as soon as you opened it.

The same essence greeted us every evening years ago, along with your whistled code, as Didi and I raced each other down the stairs to let you in after work. You would be awake for hours each night after we went to sleep, correcting tutorials, completing conference papers, finishing a painting, writing a poem. I never knew when you came to bed, but even in my dreams I'd get a whiff of that Ma smell when you vigorously rubbed Nivea on our sleep-heavy faces. I could feel its embrace so strongly the night you slipped away, as I held you close. While Didi and I sang you your favourite Tagore songs, your fragrance wrapped us up in all its tenderness.

You're the one who taught us to love songs, and to love books. Our growing-up years were filled with poetry festivals and book fairs, rather than animation films and amusement parks. And while I complained about that as a child, because of you, poetry became a lifelong ally. Watching you write and rewrite every line of your work, I was captivated by the process of editing books, which turned into my first career.

You and I loved every one of our literary projects together. When we were translating your poems in my college dormitory, you relished my stash of instant hot chocolate almost as much as our heated arguments over each word, late into the night. Years later, on your 75th birthday, I was thrilled to see your face light up when you unwrapped your surprise gift, a published copy of my translation of your latest book of poetry, *Make Up*

131

Your Mind. Just ten days before you died, we received the cover design of our dream project, *Acrobat*. You had chosen the image, a Tagore painting, with meticulous care, though the manuscript was yet to be written. With your famously dazzling smile, undiminished by illness, you exclaimed, "This is my first book to be published by a truly international press—I'm definitely going to stick around for this one!"

Although there were unending demands on your time, a few years ago you had somehow managed to find several days for us to translate together my bedtime book for children, *Not Yet!*. The book is a playful dialogue in rhyme between a mother and a child: a naughty little girl finds countless excuses not to go to bed, while her ever-patient mother is determined to put her to sleep. The literal Bengali translation of 'Not Yet' is 'Ekhoni Na', but you had laughed your own little-girl laugh and declared, "No, the girl must be much more emphatic! She will say, 'Ekkhuni na! Ekkhuni na!'" Well, this obstinate daughter of yours kept saying to her mother in the last few weeks, "Ekkhuni na, ekkhuni na . . ." Could you hear me, Ma?

Not too long ago, I pulled a big blue book from our Kolkata shelf, *365 Bedtime Stories*. When I opened it, out fell a red-gold rush of leaves—oaks, maples and ferns collected in London when I was a toddler. We had gathered them together in the woods at the bottom of the hill where we lived. One night, as you were reading to me about Tinker Bell, I interrupted you with a technical question. "What are fairy wings made of? Butterfly wings? Bird feathers? Or huge petals?" "There are all kinds of fairies, you see," you replied, "just as there are all kinds of people!" "Do all fairies look like you?" I persisted. "I don't think so," you smiled. "Fairies are very, very beautiful." "But Ma," I protested, "you're the most beautiful person in the world!" You laughed—much more raucously than Tinker Bell would—as you drew heavy curtains over tall windows. "Every little girl believes that about her mother, Toompush."

Well, Ma, I've grown up a bit. My world has grown up a lot. I left home as a child, and made beautiful friends who became my family. In my work, I've met many beautiful faces, walked with beautiful figures. I've fallen in love with beautiful minds.

You grew up too. More books published, many awards won. A few more clashes with your stubbornly loving daughters. Around your eyes, a few more lines, celebrating years of full-throated life. A few more world tours—many with me, when you swept me away with your limitless appetite for discovery, your infectious sense of wonder. Remember that list we made some years ago of unvisited countries that you absolutely had to explore? Wheelchair in tow, we made it to most entries on that list—China, Egypt, South Africa (but not Myanmar). Each time we travelled, you transformed our adventures into provocative essays or bestselling books. And on every trip, we shared even more pleasures together than our plentiful arguments. Yes, we did have fights. I cried when you didn't understand. I begged you not to nag. I yelled at you when I was upset with someone else. I watched, in panic, as tears welled up in your ever-adolescent eyes.

But I am as sure today as I was that night in London that, even if you had not been my mother, even if that most precious accident of birth had by rights been the beginning of someone else's story, even if I'd met you in any of your other roles—as a poet, professor, painter, friend, or a stranger on a plane—you would still be the most beautiful person I could ever have met.

At the end of *Not Yet!* the daughter asks, "Ma, did you turn out the light?" And the mother replies, "Yes, my dear. Now, goodnight."

—Nandana Dev Sen

Chronology

1957–1959

First Confidence   প্রথম প্রত্যয়

Mountain   পাহাড়

The Last Act   শেষ অঙ্ক

The Lie   মিথ্যে

There Was a Time   একদা

1960–1969

A sad song about words   হায় শব্দ

All those crazy blue hills   যত নীল পাগল পাহাড়

Antara   অন্তরা – ১

Heartbeat   স্পন্দন

Puppet   পুনশ্চ পুতুল

Sometimes, Love   কখনো ভালোবাসা

Sparrow, Again   আবার চড়ুই

Telephone   টেলিফোন

That Invisible Tower   তুমি ওই অদৃশ্য মিনারে

The Emperor's New Clothes

The Great Fair   রথের মেলায়

The Ocean   সমুদ্র

The Twittering Machine

These Beloved Faces   এই প্রিয় মুখগুলি মেঘের মতন

This Child   অন্তরা – ৫

1970–1979

A Night Drink

Children

Childspeak   বালভাষিতম্

Green Salad for My Husband

I Give to Baser Life   দেবতার কাল – ২

Out of Reach   ভালোবাসা – ১২

Renunciation   বন্যা

Return of the Dead   আমাকে তবে গ্রহণ করো, কলকাতা

135

Right Now: Forever   এইকাল: চিরকাল
The Jungle Story   আরণ্যক
The Last Gust   শীতঝড় ১৯৭১
The Shell
The Yellow River   ইয়াং সি কিয়াং

1980–1989

And Yet, Life   তবুও, জীবন
Chained   শুধু
Face to Face   মুখোমুখি
Full Moon Nightscape   পূর্ণিমারাত্রের দৃশ্য
In Marriage   পাণিগ্রহণ
Metamorphosis   গ্রেগর সামসার মতো একদিন
Poem on My Birthday   জন্মদিনের কবিতা
The Appointment   সময়: যৌবনকাল, ঠিকানা: পৃথিবী
The Doctor   ডাক্তার
Umbilical Cord   নাড়ী

1990–1999

A Birthday Voodoo
A Poem for My Lover   ভালোবাসা – ১
Cloud   মেঘ
Conversations, Bellagio Center
    I'm fine
    So that
December 1992   আসাম, ১৯৮০
Festival   উৎসব ১৯৯২
Too Much   ভালোবাসা – ৬
That Girl   মেয়েটা
The Lamp   বাতিটা
The Last Gust   শীতঝড় ১৯৭১ [Bengali translation]

2000–2009

A house, the colour of pain   দুঃখরঙের বাড়ি – এক
Acrobat   মাদারি

136

![Juggernaut logo]

juggernaut

THE APP
FOR INDIAN
READERS

*Fresh, original books tailored for
mobile and for India. Starting at ₹10.*

juggernaut.in

1

CRAFTED FOR MOBILE READING

Thought you would never read a book on mobile? Let us prove you wrong.

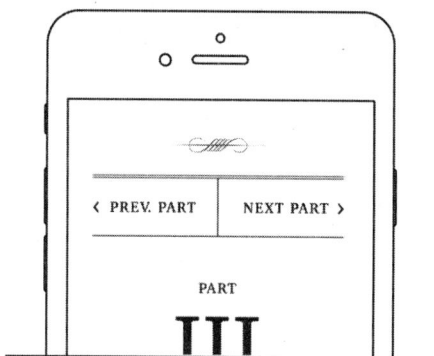

Beautiful Typography

The quality of print transferred
to your mobile. Forget ugly PDFs.

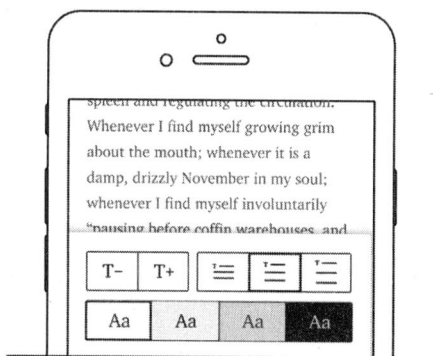

Customizable Reading

Read in the font size, spacing
and background of your liking.

2

❋

AN EXTENSIVE LIBRARY

Including fresh, new, original Juggernaut books from the likes of Sunny Leone, Praveen Swami, Husain Haqqani, Umera Ahmed, Rujuta Diwekar and lots more. Plus, books from partner publishers and loads of free classics. Whichever genre you like, there's a book waiting for you.

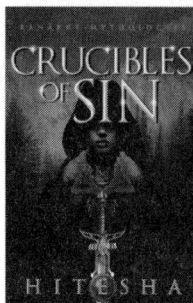

CRUCIBLES OF SIN
HITESHA

Can a Geek ever find Love?
Finding Juliet
Toffee

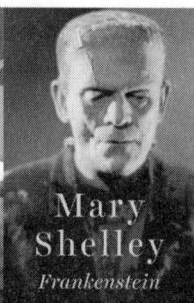

Mary Shelley
Frankenstein

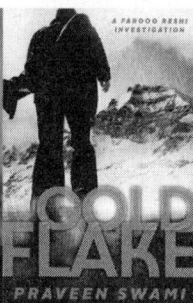

A FAROOQ REHSI INVESTIGATION
GOLD FLAKE
PRAVEEN SWAMI

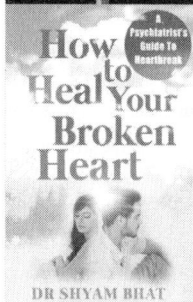

A Psychiatrist's Guide To Heartbreak
How to Heal Your Broken Heart
DR SHYAM BHAT

MOIN AND THE MONSTER

Stories of women from Mumbai
S. Hussain Zaidi
with Jane Borges
Foreword by Vishal Bharadwaj

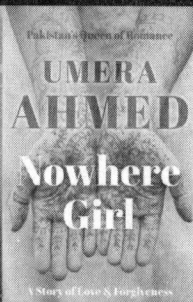

Pakistan's Queen of Romance
UMERA AHMED
Nowhere Girl
A Story of Love & Forgiveness

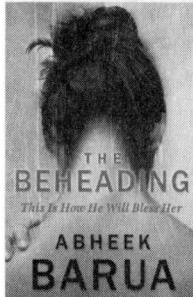

THE BEHEADING
This Is How He Will Bless Her
ABHEEK BARUA

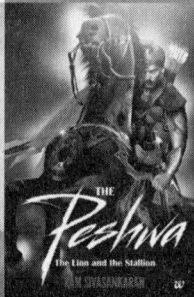

THE Peshwa
The Lion and the Stallion
RAM SIVASANKARAN

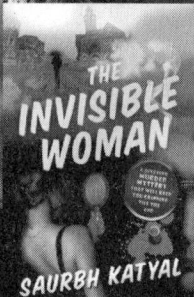

THE INVISIBLE WOMAN
SAURBH KATYAL

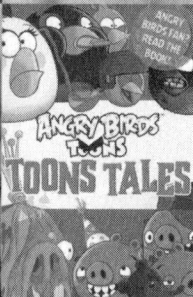

ANGRY BIRDS? READ THE BOOK
ANGRY BIRDS TOONS TALES

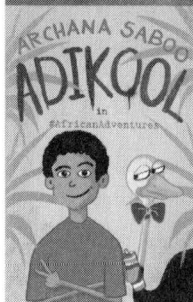

ARCHANA SABOO
ADIKOOL
in #AfricanAdventures

i am not a bimbette
Tarana Khan

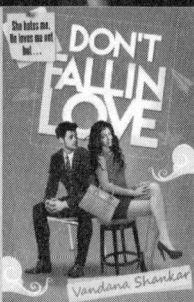

She hates me. He loves me not ...
DON'T FALL IN LOVE
Vandana Shankar

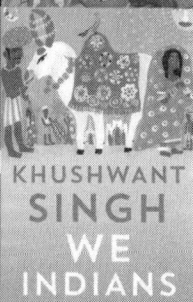

KHUSHWANT SINGH
WE INDIANS

DON'T JUST READ; INTERACT

We're changing the reading experience from passive to active.

Ask authors questions

Get all your answers from the horse's mouth.
Juggernaut authors actually reply to every
question they can.

Rate and review

Let everyone know of your favourite reads or
critique the finer points of a book – you will be
heard in a community of like-minded readers.

Gift books to friends

For a book-lover, there's no nicer gift than
a book personally picked. You can even
do it anonymously if you like.

Enjoy new book formats

Discover serials released in parts over
time, picture books including comics,
and story-bundles at discounted rates.
And coming soon, audiobooks.

4

LOWEST PRICES & ONE-TAP BUYING

Books start at ₹10 with regular discounts and free previews.

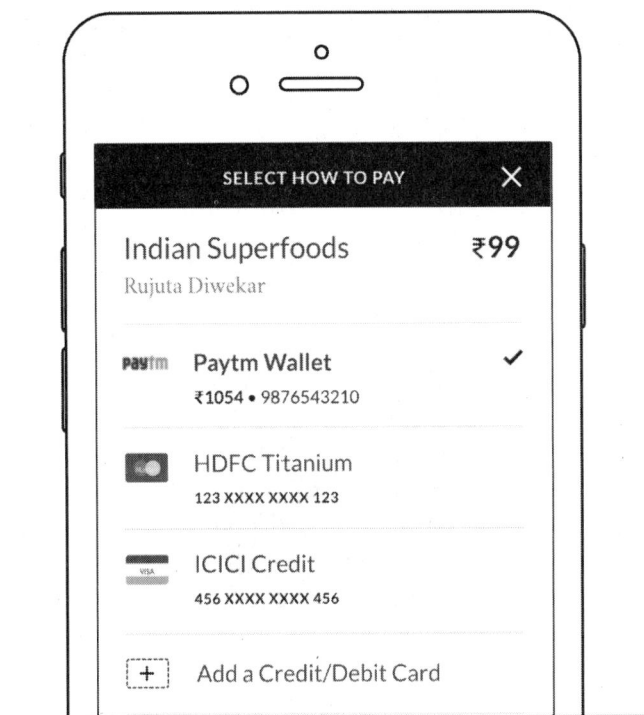

SELECT HOW TO PAY ✕

Indian Superfoods   ₹99
Rujuta Diwekar

paytm   **Paytm Wallet**   ✓
         ₹1054 • 9876543210

         ICICI Credit
         123 XXXX XXXX 123

         ICICI Credit
         456 XXXX XXXX 456

   [+] Add a Credit/Debit Card

Paytm Wallet, Cards & Apple Payments

On Android, just add a Paytm Wallet once and buy any book with one tap. On iOS, pay with one tap with your iTunes-linked debit/credit card.

To download the app scan the QR Code
with a QR scanner app

For our complete catalogue, visit www.juggernaut.in
To submit your book, send a synopsis and two
sample chapters to books@juggernaut.in
For all other queries, write to contact@juggernaut.in